Sheffield's Evolution

Sheffield is situated on the foothills of the [Pennines]. [It is] founded upon seven hills, and its water sup[ply is good. The main] river is called the Don (Once pronounced t[he Dun), with tributaries] from the rivers - Loxely, Rivelin, Porter an[d Sheaf. Sheffield is] very hilly due to the series of ridges and cross-valleys.

Before the Doomsday book, Sheffield's history is very vague. At Wincobank there are the remains of an Iron-age fort. The city did not start to develop until the 12th century, when a Norman castle was sited at the joining of the rivers Don and Sheaf. This castle was a wooden Motte and Bailey type.
The one that replaced it in 1270 was stone built, and was badly damaged during the English Civil War of 1648. The castle has since been demolished but its foundations are still intact under the "Castle Market". The Norman's also built the first parish church where the present day Anglican Cathedral of St Peter & St Paul now stands.

In 1297, as industry started to grow, the Furnival Charter granted some civic self-government.

Some of Sheffield's street names still echo the Medieval layout. Look in particular for - Furnival Gate, Fargate, Haymarket, and Westbar.

The Wicker area was once used for archery Practice, and it was near here that witches were "Tried" on the river using a "Ducking stool".

Cathedral of St Peter & St Paul

Sheffield was an ideal place to start a steel and cutlery industry due to the abundant natural resources of coal, sandstone, ironstone and timber. It also had five fast flowing rivers. Water powered hamlets soon developed along these rivers. Some of these hamlet sites still remain intact and working today.

Between the years 1570 and 1584, Mary Queen of Scots was held prisoner in Sheffield's castle, and the Turret House at Manor Lodge.

During the civil war, the royalists captured Sheffield castle, but with local help the parliamentary forces managed to expel them. The castle was later demolished and its stone used to construct and adorn many of Sheffield's buildings.

The Winter Garden – Visitor Information
Call – 0114) 221 1900 (Admission Free – 364 days a year)

Sheffield's Evolution

In 1624, an Act of Parliament had set up a "Company of Cutlers" to oversee the industry in Hallamshire and county of York. The "Cutlers Hall" building on Church Street was built in 1832, and is a grade 2 listed building. It is Sheffield's third Cutlers Hall. The previous buildings, which were built in the same location, were constructed in 1638 and 1725.

By 1742, steel production was flourishing in Sheffield, but no more than 200 tons of "shear steel" were being produced each year. Benjamin Huntsman changed this by inventing the crucible method of making steel. A100 years later, Sheffield had increased its yearly production of crucible steel to 20,000 tons. At the time it was approximately 40% of Europe's total steel production.

In 1743, Thomas Boulsover invented Old Sheffield Plate. It was a mistake he made whilst repairing a knife handle that caused the fusing of the silver with the copper. The end result was a silver exterior at a fraction of the cost. The craftsmen soon started to produce fashionable tableware and decorative ornaments from this new material. (Examples of this metalwork can be seen in the Millennium Galleries).

By the mid 1700's, Sheffield had a population of almost 10,000 people. This increased to around 45,000 by the start of the 1800's. Properties were built and extended in order to cope with the new influx of people entering the town. Civil unrest at that time was high over the enclosure of land and recruiting for the French wars. Radical attitudes and the suppression of newspapers caused rioting in the area. The authorities responded by building a barracks at Hillsborough to maintain law and order.

Around 1820, there was a trade revival, and Charities were busy setting up public schools, Hospitals and dispensaries, whilst companies And shareholders were investing in colleges And botanical gardens.

Meanwhile, quality of life for the workingman Was getting worse. Poor water, sewage and Polluted air, were a major contributor to the Cholera epidemic that killed 402 people in 1832.

Hillsborough Barracks

Sheffield City Hall – Enquiries – (0114) 2233 740 / 1

Sheffield's Evolution

By 1855, steel was in great demand for the railways and military armour plate. To meet that need Henry Bessemer devised the new "Converter" process that produced large steel volumes at a much cheaper price. Soon factories along the Don Valley were making all types of steel products, but this came to an abrupt halt on the night of March 11th 1864, when the newly constructed Dale Dyke Dam gave way. Millions of gallons of water raced down the Loxley Valley through Hillsborough, and flooded the valley with the loss of 248 lives.

In 1873, cheap transport in the form of electric Tramcars were introduced. By 1903, there were 281 miles of track and the maximum fare was One penny. The last old Sheffield tramcar ran Until 1960, when it went to Thomas W. Ward To be dismantled.
In 1893, Sheffield achieved city status, and Later in 1897, the Town Hall was opened by Queen Victoria.

Steel Making

During the 2nd World War, Sheffield was attacked as Hitler recognised that the city was producing high-speed steels, munitions, and forging crankshafts for Spitfire engines. On the 12th and 15th of December 1940, there were two massive bombing raids which killed nearly 700 people. This became known as the "Sheffield Blitz". After the war the rebuilding of homes and industry began. Buses replaced the trams and high-rise blocks of flats were built. The introduction of the "Clean Air Act" started to transform Sheffield into a very clean city. Sheffield University was established in 1905, and later in 1992, the Hallam University became Sheffield's second.

On the 21st March 1994, the Supertram system opened across the city. The full network route of 29km was completed on 23rd of October 1995.

Present day Sheffield is highly diversified with popular music venues, sports stadiums, learning and technology centres and its specialist steel products. The city is also recognised for Bassett's (Liquorice Allsorts), Henderson's "brown-black" Relish, and the Full Monty (Film). It is also the birthplace of many famous people – Michael Palin, Joe Cocker, Pulp, Human league, and Def Leopard to name a few. We hope you enjoy using this book as a fun way to explore the city and its historic past.

Dialect: "Shutyergob" translates to "Be quiet"
"Thacandooitthesen" translates to "Do it yourself"

Reflections

When I was a boy, I never really thought about the city I lived in, and for me the Botanical Gardens was my whole world. Times were hard and we children had to be content with simple pleasures. I was fortunate that the Botanical Gardens were nearby, free to enter, and full of exciting things to see and do. Sometimes on my way home from Hunters Bar School, I would go to the gardens to see the scarlet macaws. On one occasion a macaw pecked off all the buttons on my duffle coat – but I thought that was great! I would also visit the bear pit, the fossilised tree and my favourite – "Peter Pan" (Pan spirit of the woods) in the Rose Garden. There was always something interesting to tell my mother when I got home.

I missed the gardens when our family moved to Walkley. The terraced housed streets were now my new play area. I soon found the corner shop was where people gossiped about the latest news and created long delays in getting served. The Fine Fare and PriceKeene at Crookes were the biggest shops around. Town was generally used only for large purchases, but we would sometimes go late on Friday night to Dixon Lane's "Rag and Tag" market. The butcher's shops had no refrigerators to keep the meat in over the weekend, and they would give their last customers "extra meat" just to get rid of it.

Our ride home on the tram to School Road was often after a long wait as several would pass by full. I remember getting dust on my coat from a grinder or steelworker, as they brushed past to get to a seat. The sign inside the tram that said "No Spitting" always amused me, as it was common then for workingmen to chew tobacco and spit it out.
I cried as I sat on the very last tram as it went to Thomas W. Ward ltd. to be dismantled.

In Sheffield's centre was the Goodwin fountain with illuminated water jets at the junction of Fargate and Surrey Street, and at the High Street and Haymarket junction was the "Hole in the Road". This was a subterranean underpass and featured a large fish tank that once held Piranha's. In 1977, I remember the Town hall extension being built. The building's radical design soon earned it the nickname of "The Egg Box". All of these "features" were removed over the years, but the Goodwin fountain has since been rebuilt in the Peace Gardens with its 89 "walk in" jets.

Like other teenagers I enjoyed the nightlife in Sheffield around the 70's and 80's which included famous venues like - The Roxy, The Fiesta, The Genevieve nightclub, The Wappentake Bar, Bailey's night club, The Hofbrauhaus Bavarian beer Keller, and The Black Swan. Top performing artists visited Sheffield's show clubs and the admission dress code was very strict. Wearing a tie or having one rolled up in your pocket was an item you dared not forget if you wanted to enter a nightclub after pub closing time.
Popular city centre cinemas around this time included the Gaumont, Odeon, ABC, and The Classic, which was in Fitzalan Square.

Sheffield as Britain's 4th largest city is still going through changes, and for me over the last forty years - it's hard to remember them all!

Yer tellem that today, an they waint believe yer!

The Quick Quiz

20 Easier questions to suit younger readers.
(Answers are on page 47)

Your Rating: -   5-10 - Improvement needed   11-15 – Good
16-19 – Very Good   20 - Excellent   21 – Awesome

#	Question	Answer
1	Sheffield Wednesday Football Club nickname?	
2	Sheffield United Football Club's nickname?	
3	The Sheffield's Speedway team is called?	
4	What sport does the Sheffield Steelers play?	
5	Does Ponds Forge make metal, or is it for swimming?	
6	What is the complex at Meadowhall mainly used for?	
7	Is Henderson's Relish - yellow or black in colour?	
8	The "Full XXXXX " was filmed in Sheffield	
9	What theatre in Sheffield hosts world snooker?	
10	Which transport operator runs Supertram?	
11	What park has a rare breeds centre in it?	
12	What type of "Allsorts" are Bassett's famous for?	
13	Which is the older building - the City or Town Hall?	
14	Who invented Old Sheffield Plate?	
15	What animal was kept in Botanical Garden's pit?	
16	How many road tiers / levels are on Tinsley Viaduct?	
17	Which queen opened the Town Hall in 1897?	
18	Meadowhall is next to which M1 Motorway junction?	
19	Which Sheffield band is Jarvis Cocker a member of?	
20	What is Sheffield's Basketball team's nickname?	

Tie Breaker: Which year did Sheffield Airport open?

**Parks, Woodlands and Countryside Ranger Service
For a calendar of events call - (0114) 250 0500**

The City Centre Quest

Sheffield city centre has many points of interest and your quest is to collect the 30 answers whilst visiting some of these places. Your Quest starts at the City Hall in Barkers Pool, and is a round walk that takes approximately 2 hours. This brief map outlines the quest route. Good Luck!

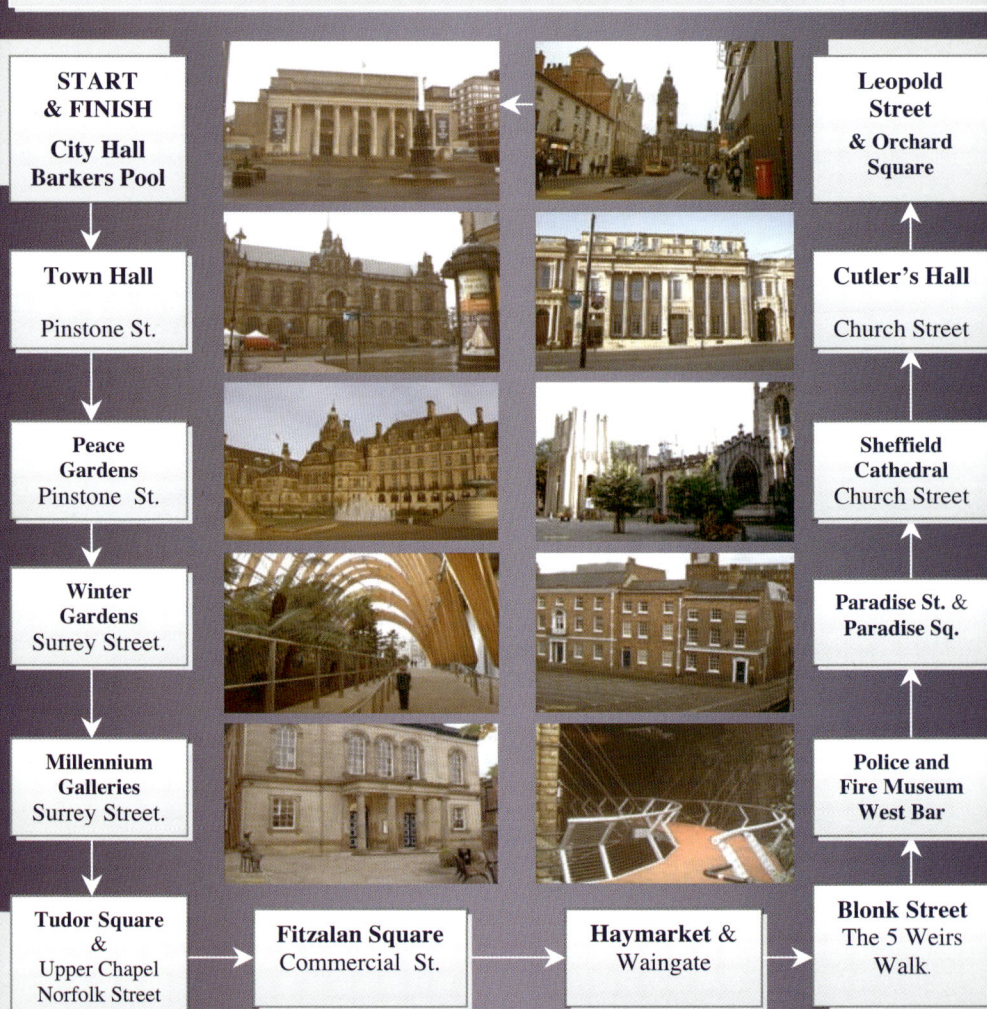

8   Answers to this quest? – please see page 47

The City Centre Quest

Your Quest:	To obtain the answers to the 30 clues
Duration:	Approximately 2 hours
Parking:	Carver Street
Equipment:	Street Map – Pen - Camera (optional)
Food/Drink:	There are bars and restaurants on the quest route
Transport:	Walking is the best way
Access:	Good all places - Note: some places close on Sundays
Answers:	Please see page 47

Start: Walk from the City Hall to the Town Hall

Q1. The City hall frontage has how many tall columns?
Q2. What is the hall called at the back of the City Hall?
Q3. What police item is found next to the Town Hall?

Info: Sheffield became a city in 1893.
Queen Victoria opened the Town Hall in 1897.
Next: Please proceed to the Peace Gardens.

A1.

A2.

A3.

Start: The Peace Gardens

Q4. Who is the Chartist leader on the wall plaque?
Q5. What Japanese city is remembered here?
Q6. Which German city presented the "Ships bell?

Info: The Peace Garden's were originally called Saint Paul's Gardens. The name formerly changed in 1985.
Next: Please proceed to The Winter Gardens.

A4.

A5.

A6.

Start: The Winter Garden / Millennium Galleries

Q7. The Winter Garden opened officially on what date?
Q8. The bronze figure at the building front is called?
Q9. The Millennium galleries opened in what year?

Info: The Winter Gardens was open to the public on 12-12-02. The official opening came later by the Queen.
Next: Please proceed to Tudor Square

A7.

A8.

A9.

The Millennium Galleries – Tel: – (0114) 278 2600

The City Centre Quest

Start: Tudor Square

Q10. What two theatres are found in Tudor Square?
Q11. Who is featured on a plaque with dates 1705-1788?
Q12. Which Sheffield mayor is mentioned on a plaque?
Info: There is a wall plaque on the City Library that has the information you seek.
Next: Please proceed to Fitzalan Square

A10.

A11.

A12.

Start: Fitzalan Square

Q13. The statue is to commemorate which king?
Q14. What signature is on the "fame and truth" plaque?
Q15. What was the large stone built "listed" building?
Info: The cinema in Fitzalan Square was called "The Classic" – It is now an amusement arcade.
Next: Please proceed to the Haymarket

A13.

A14.

A15.

Start: Haymarket and Waingate

Q16. Which house has a "man" hung high on the wall?
Q17. On Castle Street is a large wall picture. What has the man got on his head?
Q18. At the bottom of Waingate is an old brewery (Whitbread beers) What is it called?
Next: Please proceed to Blonk St. and the 5 Weir Walk

A16.

A17.

A18.

Start: The 5 Weir Walk at Smithfield's

Q19. What date is on the cross just before the bridge?
Q20. What colour floor is seen on "Cobweb Bridge"?
Q21. How many spiders are under the bridge archway?
Info: The Five Weir Quest is featured in this book.
Next: Please proceed to West Bar along Bridge Street.

A19.

A20.

A21.

Factoid: Lady's Bridge is so named because of a chapel "Of our Lady" that was built near to the bridge.

The City Centre Quest

Start: West Bar and Paradise Square

Q22. What museum is found at West Bar roundabout?

Q23. Who once preached in Paradise Square?

Q24. What is the name of the "Row" at the side of the Cathedral? (Proceed up the Row to access the Cathedral)

Info: Paradise Square has a plaque-seek it out.
Next: Please enter Sheffield's Cathedral.

A22.

A23.

A24.

Start: The Cathedral of St.Peter and St.Paul

Q25. What year is found on the bell of HMS Sheffield?

Q26. The 6th Earl of Shrewsbury died in which year?

Q27. The East wall, has stones from which centuries?

Info: The Lantern Tower roof glass represents the "Crown of thorns". (Entering on the west side).
Next: Please proceed to Cutler's Hall on Church Street.

A25.

A26.

A27.

Start: Cutler's Hall – Church Street

Q28. What year was the Company of Cutlers founded?

Q29. The present hall was built in what year?

Q30. What are the front entrance doors made of?

Quest End: Please return to The City Hall along Leopold Street. (Turn right into Barkers Pool.)

Info: Leopold Street was named after King Leopold.

A28.

A29.

A30.

The City Hall was built in 1932, and is a popular venue for music, dancing and Christmas pantomimes. The building next to the City Hall (shown right) was formerly the Sheffield Water Works Company. (The year it was built is high on the upper stonework)

S.S.Electrical –   Tel: (0114) - 2580542
For all your Electrical and Security needs.

City Information

Emergency calls - Police - Fire - Ambulance   999
(On a mobile phone network call - 112)

Sheffield / South Yorkshire. Police	(0114) 220 2020
Crime stoppers	**0800 555 111**
South Yorks. – Fire and Rescue	(0114) 27 27 202
Yorkshire Electricity - 24HR	0800 375675
Gas - Transco - (Gas emergency service)	0800 111 999
Water - Yorkshire Water	0845 124 2424
Environmental Emergencies	0800 807 060
Floodline	0845 988 1188
RSPCA - (24hr) Help line	0870 555 5999
NHS Direct	0845 46 47
Northern General – A+E only	(0114) 243 4343
Royal Hallamshire Hospital	(0114) 271 1900
Children's Hospital	(0114) 271 7000
Sheffield - Town Hall	(0114) 272 6444
Travellers with Disabilities	(0114) 276 6148
Shopmobility - Sheffield	(0114) 281 2278
Meadowhall	0845 600 6800
Rotherham	(01709) 517100
Transport: Sheffield Airport / Pleasure Flights	(0114) 201 1998
British Rail	08457 48 49 50
S.Y. Traveline / enquiries	01709 51 51 51
National Traveline / enquiries	0870 608 26 08
Sheffield tourist Information	(0114) 221 1900
Sheffield Countryside Service	(0114) 250 0500
Mobile Library Service	(0114) 273 4277
Consumer Advice	(0114) 273 6289

The Five Weirs Quest

Your Quest: To travel along the Five Weirs Walk obtaining the Answers to the 25 clues.   (It is well signposted)
Time to do: Approximately 4 – 5 hours
Terrain: Footpaths could become muddy after rain – Cycles permitted
Distance: 8 Kilometres   **Access:**   Disabled access provided

Information

Your quest will take you along the River Don and past five weirs to end at Meadowhall. The walk takes you past Victorian buildings, mills, factories, and schools. It is easy to imagine what it was like when it was the city's industrial heyday. The experience is quite unique as the industrial relics are fused with nature and the abundant wildlife. At certain sites along the footpath there are information boards that tell you of historic points of interest. An alternative route could be to start at Meadowhall, and return by bus.

Your quest will be over when all the questions are answered.   (Answers Page 46)

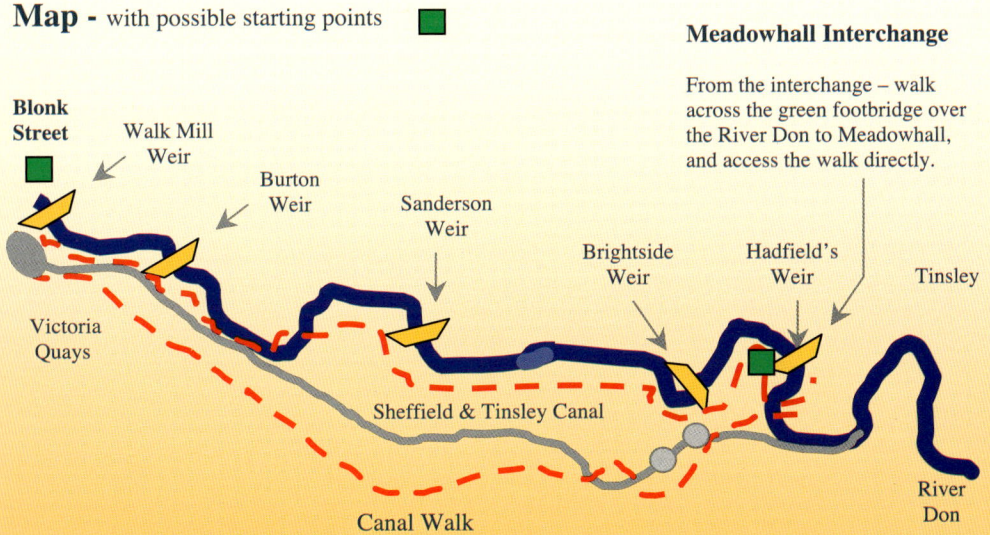

Map - with possible starting points

Graves Art Gallery – Call (0114) 278 2600
Surrey Street - Sheffield 1

13

The Five Weirs Quest

The clues start from the Five Weirs Walk entrance on Blonk Street. There is a Parking facility on nearby Broad Street. This is free on Sundays (Please check). Approximate progress timings will be given after each set of clues. (The answers are on page 46)

1	What Queen is named in the City Centre Quay title?	
2	What is the name of the weir nearest to Lady's Bridge? (Map of walk on bridge)	
3	What is the date on the Five Weirs Cross at Smithfield's entrance?	
4	What butterfly is shown on the Wicker Riverside information board?	
5	What is the name of the bridge - shown in the picture below? (Seek a plaque)	

This bridge is supported from the sidewalls of the arch. The River Don is below you. Be sure to look upwards as you pass along the bridge.
Follow the walk signs to the next set of clues.

14   **Victoria Quays** - Once Sheffield's canal basin, has specialist shops, hotels, restored warehouses and more.

The Five Weirs Quest

You are approximately 30 minutes from the starting point. The quest continues along Effingham Street and along the River Don towards Salmon Pastures. This section has some interesting industrial buildings and bridges. Watch out for wildlife, herons and Kingfishers, plus the carved benches as you walk towards Washford Bridge.

6	How many metal spiders are hanging from the roof of the bridge?	
7	What is the full name of the company shown in the logo below?	
8	You need to find when Norfolk Bridge was built? (Seek a plaque)	
9	What creature is carved into the benches at Salmon Pastures?	
10	What is the date shown on the school dedication stone at Salmon Pastures?	

Q7.   Who's Logo?

This company started in the early 1870's when there was a great demand for scrap metal. The company quickly expanded to be probably the largest scrap dealers in the country. Amongst other ventures was ship dismantling, which started in 1894. During the war, it was said that the business leased an elephant called Lizzie to help move heavy loads. In 1960 the last Sheffield tram ended here. The firm continued until the early 1980's.

Factoid: 402 people died in the Sheffield Cholera epidemic of 1832 – On Norfolk Road, there is a 7 metre high memorial.

15

The Five Weirs Quest

You are about 60 minutes away from the starting point. This section has a seated viewing platform. It is a good place for a short rest if required.

11 What two year numbers are carved into the wood bench near Washford Bridge?

12 What is the name of the steel and file-maker shown on the information board at Salmon Pastures / Washford Bridge?

13 On the Five Weirs Walk Bridge plaque How far is it to East Coast Road, and Brightside Lane?

Burton weir

Old riverside factories

The new Bailey bridge on Effingham Street Spanning the River Don.

16 Botanical Gardens – Call – 0114 267 6496
Admission free – open daily

The Five Weirs Quest

14	What two fish are mentioned at Royd's Mill information board?	
15	Which lord of the manor had Sanderson's weir constructed?	
16	Who established the Hecla Works?	
17	What relic of WWII is mentioned on the Hecla information board?	
18	What is the name of the bridge in the final section of the Don valley link road?	

You are about 90 minutes from the starting point. The next section of the walk takes you towards Sanderson's weir and the Hecla Works.

Hint: After getting the bridge information, turn towards Attercliffe Common. You need to turn down Carbrooke Street to rejoin the walk.

The River Don at Hecla Works

Brightside Weir

Factoid: Park Hill flats were built from 1955 to 1961.

The Five Weirs Quest

You are now approximately 2.5 hours from the starting point. The walk continues along Attercliffe Road for a short while, and passes some good stops for food and drink. You then pass the Forgemasters building and turn left down Carbrooke Street. Nearby Carbrooke Hall (pub) was once used by the parliamentarians in the civil war, and is reputed to be haunted.

19 What steel bird is seen on the left, as you enter the Brightside walk entrance?

20 Which weir is the largest of the five that are listed on the five weirs walk?

21 At Meadowhall, cross the River Don using the green bridge. Which company erected this bridge? (Seek a plaque)

22 How many large support wires are there on the new enclosed Interchange Bridge to Meadowhall's shopping area?
(Count both sides)

At the bottom of Broughton Lane, is the Noose and Gibbet - public house. Outside the pub front is a hanging cage, which recreates the sentence imposed on Spence Broughton for robbing the Sheffield Mail coach. It is said that the body was on display there for 27 years as a deterrent to other highwaymen.

18 Factoid: Sheffield's Supertram is powered from 750v D.C. They collect power from overhead lines using a pantograph.

The Five Weirs Quest

You are approximately 4 hours away from the starting point by now. (The final clues are below. The answers are on Page 46).

This section of the Don Valley was the target for German bombers during WWII, as the Vickers works had the only drop hammer at the time capable of forging crankshafts for spitfire engines.
The Hadfield's works produced specialised munitions.

Germany made two major air attacks on the area on the nights of the 12th and 15th of December 1940. Bombs were dropped from over 300 aircraft, and the raids lasted for almost nine hours. These extensive raids on Sheffield became known as the "Sheffield Blitz".

Today the area is acknowledged as a centre for sports, music, shopping, cinemas, bowling and entertainment.

Your quest concludes now. Further quests are on our website below.

23	What three means of transport are displayed on the Meadowhall interchange sign?	
24	How many road levels are there on the Tinsley Viaduct?	
25	How many large cooling towers are there at Tinsley next to the viaduct?	

Factoid: Sheffield Wednesday's first match was on 31-12-1867 They played Dronfield F.C.

19

The Cryptic Quiz

This quiz is compiled from cryptic clues that relate to Sheffield and its district names. i.e. Heeley   (The answers are listed on page 47.)

1) Optimists could live here?
2) Poachers can get a drink here perhaps?
3) A Motorbike for this Sheffield area?
4) "Murderous Swamp" in the Sheffield area
5) You can shop at this place that has chairs made of timber.
6) It is the centre place for many trees that are placed to the left and to the right of it.
7) A person who cuts their privet too much will end up with this Sheffield area.
8) Not another tree could be planted here?
9) You can buy most things at this place - even mountains of expensive glass.
10) "Shake a bell gently" in this Sheffield Area
11) Set fire to mourner? In this Sheffield Area.
12) Western side of Sheffield for Swindlers - if you believe the areas name!
13) Mining shafts in a wide-open area?
14) Environmentally friendly steep incline.
15) Area and river in Sheffield that gave Robin Hood his full title perhaps?
16) Repairs every piece of clothing with thread
17) Company deposits a windfall into a financial institution?
18) Place for an annoyed vicar?

Factoid: HMS Sheffield's crew sang "Always look on the bright side of life" whilst the ship was sinking after the missile attack.

The Car Quest

The Car Quest is a circular tour around Sheffield's places of interest. It will take approximately 5 hours to complete. Along the way are stops where meals and drinks are available. (See the information box next to the clues). The quest could be set under competition rules where the winner is the car that has the highest correct number of answers and has taken the least time. (Large A4 quest sheets are available on our website). Alternatively, you can visit the places at your leisure, as there is much to see and explore at each venue.

Remember - Be safe and keep to national speed limits.

The Quest start and end is:	**Graves Park Rare Breeds Car Park** Hemsworth Road entrance – at Norton.
Approximate circuit time is:	5-6 Hours
Approximate distance to travel:	30 Miles
Access:	Easy to all sites
Equipment:	Binoculars may help -Pen essential.
Places are listed in order of the clues	(19 clues in all).

Graves Park, Abbeydale Industrial Hamlet, Dore Village, Hunters Bar, Endcliffe Park, Weston Park, Manor Lodge, Norfolk Park and returning back to Graves Park.

Good Luck! (Answers are on page 46 or on: - www.soyouknow.co.uk)

Location: Graves Park Rare Breed Centre Hemsworth Road Entrance - car park	Time Started 00:00	
Question: What set of 3 numbers are found on the engine cover of the tractor in the Rare Breeds farm animal enclosure?	**Information:** Drinks and snack meals are available in the Rose Garden Café	
1	**Answer:**	

Carl Bullement - Accountancy – Call: 08700 850521
Free first consultation   Mobile: 07816 754 587

The Car Quest

Location:	Abbeydale Industrial Hamlet Abbeydale Road South (A621) Heading towards Totley	Time Started (00:00)	
Question: How many large supporting spokes are there on the large drive wheel of the Tilt-hammer in the entrance driveway?		**Information:** No Entrance fee is required to get this answer	
2	**Answer:**		

Location:	Dore - Village Green Battle Memorial stone Dore S17 area	Time Started (00:00)	
Question: What King of Wessex is named On the stone and what mythical creature is depicted? (Both answers required)		**Information:** You may Have to ask the locals for directions.	
3	**Answer:** **Answer:**		

Location:	Hunters Bar Roundabout Opposite Endcliffe Park Entrance	Time Started (00:00)	
Question: What is the colour and type of the gate that is situated on the roundabout, under the trees?		**Information:** There is Limited parking in the park and on the road nearby.	
4	**Answer:**		

Note: Some places listed only open on a Sunday or B/H – please check

22   **Dialect:** "Narthenthee" translates to: "Now then you"
"Shurrup" translates to: "Be quiet"

The Car Quest

| Location: | **Endcliffe Park & Woods** Ecclesall Road (A625) (Access for parking via Rustlings Road gate) | Time Started (00:00) | |

	Questions: Who carved the frog in Endcliffe Park in 1997, and what book is the frog reading? HINT: Look near the Café	Information: Drinks & Meals are available In the parks Café
5	Answer: Answer:	

| **6** | What date is mentioned on the plaque of the tree planted by Mrs George Senior? (HINT: - It's near a memorial statue) | Answer: |

| Location: | **Weston Park** Western Bank On the A57 to Lodge Moor | Time Started (00:00) | |

	Questions: Who is featured on the white memorial column in the park, and when and where was he born?	Information: The park features a working weather station
7	Answer:	

| **8** | When was Weston Park purchased by the city for the people?   (Seek a plaque) | Answer: |

| **9** | In Weston Park - How many Yorkshire and Lancaster men are honoured on the memorial to the First World War? | Answer: |

Factoid: - The Millennium Square was opened on 24th March 2006 by John Prescott - (Deputy Prime Minister)

The Car Quest

10	Which radio station planted the tree near the entrance gate to Weston Park?	Answer:
11	What event does the tree commemorate in British Broadcasting?	Answer:
12	What animal is featured on top of the peaked roof on the Mappin Art Gallery?	Answer:
13	What date is above the door on the Mappin Art Gallery columned entrance?	Answer:

Location:	Heritage park – previously the Sheffield Royal Infirmary Entrance on Albert Terrace Road - off (B6079)	Time Started (00:00)	
Question: The Sheffield General (Royal) Infirmary was the first hospital to be founded in Sheffield. What year was this?		Information: Search for a wall plaque on buildings.	
14	Answer:		

15	What date is seen high up on the front of Centenary House?

Answer:

24	Factoid: - Beldon Road flats were demolished on Saturday 11-1-04 by controlled explosion.

The Car Quest

Location:	Sheffield Manor Lodge Manor Lane – off the A1635	Time Started (00:00)	
Question:	How many individual Chimneystacks are there on the Manor Turret House?	Information: Area May be locked but the Answer can be found.	
16	Answer:		

Location:	Norfolk Heritage Park Guildford Avenue - way signposted (Small car park but easy access to it)	Time Started (00:00)	
Question:	What wooden object has been Carved by schools and placed in the Park?	Information: Café that serves hot food & drinks. - Crèche.	
17	Answer:		

18 Which duke helped in the design of Norfolk Park?   Answer:

19 What year was the park open free to the public?   Answer:

Please return to Graves Park, and log your Finish time.
The answers are on page 46.

Finish Time:

Yorkshire saying: "Say nowt, hear nowt, do nowt, but if tha dus do owt – doit for thessen! "

25

Who, What, Where & When Quest

This picture quiz asks the following questions – Who, What, Where or When? To complete this quest may require some research or a visit, but that is the challenge. You could always compete against a friend for extra fun and see who can complete this quest first. The answers are on page 46 if you surrender.

WHAT - Is this called?

Hint: Abbeydale Ind. Hamlet

1.

WHEN - were these flats demolished at Beldon Road- Sheffield?

Hint: Read this book

2.

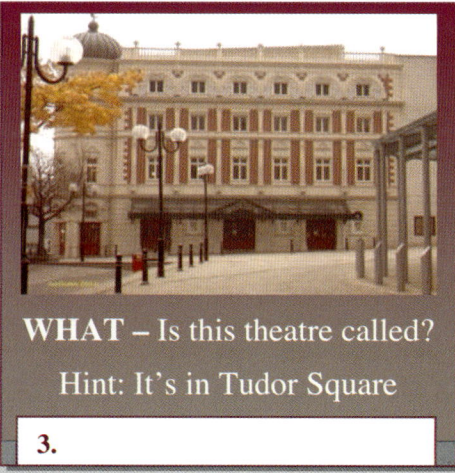

WHAT – Is this theatre called?

Hint: It's in Tudor Square

3.

WHERE – Can this be found?

Hint: In a Sheffield Park

4.

Need help? Some answers are hidden in this book, Or check out – www.soyouknow.co.uk

Who, What, Where & When Quest

WHERE – can this object be found? (Building name)
Hint: Seek a Chapel

5.

WHAT – was this place called when the Picture was taken?
Hint: Last name was "The Bed"

6.

(Left)
WHERE – can this be found?
Hint: A Square?

7.

(Right)
WHAT – is this item used to record and measure?

8.

Yorkshire saying – "Never buy owt wi wood'n andles – Cus It alus means 'ard work"

27

Who, What, Where & When Quest

WHERE – can this be Found? **Hint**: Near boats

9.

WHAT – Is the name of this main road to a famous Children's Hospital?

10.

WHO – Is this statue in Honour of?
Hint: Endcliffe Park

11.

WHO – Was the church leader that preached here to a congregation in 1779?
Hint: Paradise Square – Seek a plaque

12.

Factoid: Broadfield Road's dairy, used to have a large model of a Cow in the curved window that faced the main road.

Who, What, Where & When Quest

WHAT – Is the "Parkway's" Road "A" Number?

13.

WHO - is this at the building of the Crucible Theatre?

14.

WHAT – Is this pub called?

Hint: Look in Pond Street

15.

We hope you found this quiz entertaining. The answers are on page 46, or you can….

Visit   www.soyouknow.co.uk

* Buy these images and your Quest accessories- on line.
* Why not use this book as a Fund Raiser?
* We can design a quest to meet Your needs – Business Team Building or just for fun.
* Company advertising

Systronic Alarms - Call   (07931 58 58 50)

29

The Sheffield Word Search

This word search contains the words below that are all connected with Sheffield in some way. Double words can be halved, reversed or orientated up or down. There are no diagonals. There is a word left over – Enter this into the monthly free prize draw on our website - **www.soyouknow.co.uk**.

WORDS TO FIND:

Supertram, Ski Village, River Don, Kelham Island, Steel City, Winter Garden, Graves Park, Ponds Forge, Knives, Arena, Blades, Owls, Flood, Blitz, Vulcan, Crucible, Meadow Hall, Lyceum, Dams, Moor.

Y	T	I	C	K	G	V	M	E	A	D	O	W
W	I	N	T	E	R	U	M	U	E	C	Y	L
M	O	W	L	S	A	L	R	I	V	E	R	E
A	K	R	A	P	V	C	Z	T	I	L	B	L
R	D	A	M	S	E	A	M	O	O	R	L	B
T	M	D	K	K	S	N	X	E	K	G	A	I
R	A	N	F	L	O	O	D	G	X	A	D	C
E	H	A	R	E	N	A	X	R	K	R	E	U
P	L	L	L	L	A	H	P	O	N	D	S	R
U	E	S	T	E	E	L	K	F	X	E	K	C
S	K	I	V	I	L	L	A	G	E	N	O	D

30   THE MISSING WORD IS -

The Big Sheffield Quiz

#	Question	Answer
1	What is Sheffield United Football club's nickname?	
2	What is the name of the weir nearest to the Meadowhall shopping centre?	
3	Which is Sheffield's largest park?	
4	Which Sheffield theatre hosts World Championship Snooker?	
5	What type of laminated wood is used in the roof spans in the Winter Gardens?	
6	What sport does the Sheffield "Steeler's" participate in?	
7	What is special about the breeds of the farm animals in Graves Park?	
8	Sheffield's Airport was opened in which year?	
9	**Cryptic Clue**: A Sheffield River named after a baggage carrier?	
10	What building – (now demolished) was known locally as "The egg box"?	

Border Collie & Sheepdog Rescue
Call (0114) 2333 467 (after 6pm) "To give a dog a home"

The Big Sheffield Quiz

11 — What is Sheffield Wednesday's Football Club's nickname?

12 — What creatures are carved on the benches at Salmon Pastures?

13 — **Cryptic Clue**: (Sheffield Area) - "Supersonic recreation area"?

14 — In what year was the 1033 metre long Tinsley Viaduct opened?

15 — Which is the largest weir on the Five Weirs Walk?

16 — Annie Bindon Carter created which charity organisation?

17 — What was Samuel Holberry the leader of in Sheffield?

18 — **Cryptic Clue**: (Sheffield Area) – "Repairs everything with thread"?

19 — What two dates in December 1940 was known as the" Sheffield Blitz"?

20 — Which queen opened Sheffield's Town Hall in 1897?

32 — **Dialect:** "It'l bi reet" translates to " It will be okay"

The Big Sheffield Quiz

21	What FM. radio station is named on the Don Valley Arena?	
22	What is the date engraved on the school dedication stone at Salmon pastures?	
23	Sheffield's canal basin and buildings development are now called what?	
24	Queen Elizabeth II officially opened the Winter Gardens on what date?	
25	What film made in Sheffield, featured male strippers?	
26	Which Monty Python star was born in Sheffield in May 1943?	
27	**Cryptic Clue**: (Sheffield Area) – " Annoyed vicar "	
28	**Cryptic Clue**: (Sheffield Area) – "Dwelling made from timber"?	
29	What year was the "Sheffield Flood"?	
30	What year was HMS Sheffield sunk in the Falklands conflict?	

Meadowhall Shopping – Call – 0845 600 6800
Open daily – times vary.

The Big Sheffield Quiz

31	Which Sheffield singer "got by with a little help from his friends"?	
32	What is the name of the spider style bridge on the five weirs walk?	
33	What "A" road number is assigned to the Sheffield Parkway?	
34	What is the boxing name of Naseem Salim Ali Hamed?	
35	Who was the notable church preacher that spoke in Paradise Square on 15-7-1779?	
36	**Cryptic Clue:** (A Sheffield Area) "Murderous Swamp"?	
37	What three types of transport are shown on the Meadowhall Interchange sign?	
38	Who originated and produced a famous Sheffield Relish?	
39	How many road tiers are there on the M1 Tinsley viaduct?	
40	What is Sheffield's premier basketball team's nickname?	

34   Factoid: Orchard Square Shopping precinct opened in 1987

The Big Sheffield Quiz

41	Which Sheffield pop group sang - "Don't you want me"?	
42	What date is featured on the large cross on the five weirs walk at Smithfield's?	
43	What tree is mentioned on the Supertram stop at Manor top?	
44	What is the statue's name on top of the Town Hall's clock tower?	
45	Sheffield's cholera epidemic killed 402 people in which year?	
46	What has now replaced "The Victory Statue" in the Botanical Gardens?	
47	**Cryptic Clue:** (A Sheffield Area) "Expensive glass mountains"	
48	**Cryptic Clue:** (A Sheffield Area) "Bell shaken softly"?	
49	Botanical Gardens, was designed by its curator, who was?	
50	What is Sheffield's premier Rugby team nickname?	

Ecclesall Road – Sheffield's "golden mile" of shops

The Big Sheffield Quiz

51	What year is featured on the bell of HMS Sheffield found in Sheffield's Cathedral?	
52	What does the Lantern Tower roof in Sheffield's Cathedral represent?	
53	What year was the "Company of Cutlers" Founded in Hallam and county of York?	
54	"J. Bainbridges" shelter memorial stone - next to the Upper Chapel, is for whom?	
55	George Fullard created a statue called "The Walking man" – Where is it found?	
56	Doris Askham, held which official title when she opened Tudor Square?	
57	"Mi-Amigo" is a memorial plaque to Airmen - found in which Sheffield Park?	
58	What is the name of the fountain with 89 Jets in the Sheffield Peace Gardens?	
59	The Millennium Galleries opened in April of which Year?	
60	Sheffield F.C. was founded by Creswick and Prest in which year?	

36 Kelham Island Industrial Museum – Call (0114) 272 2106

The Big Sheffield Quiz

61	Which queen was imprisoned in Sheffield Castle and the Turret House?	
62	**Cryptic Clue**: (Sheffield Area) "Man who cuts his privet to much, ends up with this"	
63	What Sheffield square was the "Classic" Cinema to be found in?	
64	Which family, did Carbrooke Hall belong to in 1176?	
65	Which lord of the manor owned a corn mill in 1328 at Brightside?	
66	In 1875, how many acres did William Jessop's factory occupy at Brightside?	
67	What year was Weedon Street Bridge built?	
68	What type of "league" were Ian Marsh and Martyn Ware founders of?	
69	Which "Forces" used Carbrooke Hall during the Civil War of 1642-1649?	
70	The Graves Park gatehouse on Hemsworth Road, has how many chimneystacks?	

Factoid: Bishops House dates from around the 1500's, and is a museum in Meersbrook Park, at Norton Lees.

The Big Sheffield Quiz

71	The Tilt hammer's large wheel at Abbeydale industrial hamlet, has how many spokes?	
72	What colour are the "1960 date letters" above the door on Norton's water tower?	
73	What two saints are named in Sheffield Cathedral's title?	
74	What was type of tank was there in the "hole in the road" underpass? (answer in this book)	
75	Sheffield became a city in which year?	
76	Where was the "Rag and Tag" markets location in Sheffield? (Nearest lane name)	
77	What was the large item displayed in the window of Broadfield Road's Dairy?	
78	Where is the statue "Pan spirit of the woods" to be found?	
79	What animal was kept in the "pit" in the Botanical Gardens?	
80	Who is the large statue in honour of, at the Hunters Bar entrance to Endcliffe Park?	

The answers are on page 46

Cross Word

This "Cross" word has clues that are all connected with Sheffield. You have to obtain the answers then work out where the words will fit without getting "cross"- (hence the title). The number of letters for each clue answer is shown. Some starter letters have already been added.

(**Tip**: Pencil in the answers first)

Clues

* A Sheffield river   (3)
* Tragic water event   (5)
* Old Central Theatre (6)
* Town hall top statue (6)
* Sheffield metal   (5)
* Sheffield Stadium   (5)
* Old rail vehicle   (4)
* Huge water container? (3)
* Sheffield river and
  Also a bag carrier ? (6)

The solution is on page 47.

Factoid: Botanical Gardens "Pan spirit of the woods" was cast by Cashmore & Co. London.

"Part of a Picture" Quest

These pictures are "Part" of a Sheffield photograph, and your quest is to find the name of the building featured. Hints regarding the locations have been added. Should you surrender to the quest, the answers are on page 47.

1. Hint - (Arundel Gate)

2. Hint – (Pinstone Street.)

3. Hint – (Bolsover Street)

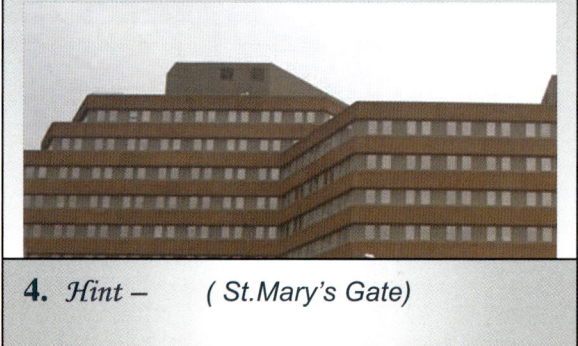

4. Hint – (St.Mary's Gate)

Most of these pictures have been taken in or near to the city centre. This Quest may take some time to complete (providing you do not look at the answers on page 47). Name the buildings to complete the Quest.
Why not compete with a friend?

Factoid: Manor Lodge – was originally a Hunting Lodge. (In the 16th Century it became a residence for the lords of the manor.)

"Part of a Picture" Quest

5. *Hint -* (Tudor Square)

6. *Hint -* (Surrey Street)

7. *Hint –* (Shalesmoor)

8. *Hint -* (Tudor Square)

9. *Hint -* (Clarkehouse Road)

10. *Hint -* (Barkers Pool)

Factoid: Park Hill flats were built in the late 1950's, and In 1998 they were made a Grade 2 listed building.

"Part of a Picture" Quest

11. *Hint -* (Old house- Manor Lane)

12. *Hint –* (Surrey Street)

13. *Hint –* (Western Bank – A57)

14. *Hint –* (Church Street)

15. *Hint –* (Church Street)

16. *Hint –* (Queens boating area?)

Answers to this Quest are on Page 47

Factoid: Francis Chantrey was a Sheffield born sculptor

Complete the pub name

Complete the names of famous or once famous Sheffield Public Houses by guessing the answer from the partially filled in clue. (Answers P.47)

Clue 1: Pub in Pond Street – (Shown left).

_ L _   _ _ E _ _ 'S   _ _ A _

Clue 2: Real Ale pub on Alma Street.

T _ _   _ _ _   _ A _

Clue 3: Old name for "The Mucky Duck".
(Now the Boardwalk)

_ _ E   _ L _ _ _   _ _ A _

Clue 4: Arundel Gate's Bavarian Beer Keller
(Now gone.)

_ _ E   _ O _ _ _ _ U _ A _ _

Clue 5: Pub famous for loud rock music.
(Now gone.)

_ _ _   _ _ P _ _ _ _ A _ E

The Fire and Police Museum – West Bar
Open Sundays and B/Hols. Call – (0114) 249 1999

"Pub Style" Quiz - 1

Twenty questions plus a tie-breaker on the subject of Sheffield.
Try this or other "Pub style" quizzes from our website:
www.soyouknow.co.uk
The quizzes are ideal for fund raising or just for fun. (Answers on Page 46)

#	Question	Answer
1	In which park can Bishop's House be found?	
2	Sir Francis Chantrey is famous for which form of art?	
3	What year were the Winter Gardens officially open?	
4	What is the Sheffield Steeler's chosen sport?	
5	What year was the City Hall built?	
6	HMS Sheffield sank in the Falklands in what year?	
7	Who designed Botanical Gardens Glass houses?	
8	Which is Sheffield's largest park?	
9	Which Sheffield area has a Spa Bath House?	
10	Which transport operator runs Supertram?	
11	What year was the Sheffield Blitz?	
12	George Wolstenholm was famous for producing what?	
13	What film featuring strippers was shot in Sheffield?	
14	Who created a famous Sheffield Relish?	
15	Which Sheffield theatre hosts World snooker?	
16	Sheffield's Michael Palin was born in what year?	
17	What was the Town hall extension's local nickname?	
18	What year was Sheffield University founded?	
19	What tragedy happened in Sheffield in 1864?	
20	Which Sheffield band made the album "Hysteria"?	
Tiebreaker	What viewer capacity has Hillsborough stadium?	

Sheffield Theatres - Call – (0114) 249 6000

"Pub Style" Quiz - 2

Twenty questions, plus a tiebreaker on Sheffield.

Try this and other "Pub style" game sheets from our website: www.soyouknow.co.uk
The quizzes are ideal for fund raising or just for fun. (Answers Page 47)

#	Question	Answer
1	What epidemic happened in Sheffield in 1832?	
2	Who was the founder of "Painted Fabrics"?	
3	Who invented the Crucible steel making method?	
4	Which year was the Don Valley stadium opened?	
5	What sport/game is played by the Sheffield Eagles?	
6	Which shopping centre was opened on 4th Sept. 1990?	
7	Who is Vance Arnold better known as?	
8	What was formed on 24th October 1857 in Sheffield?	
9	The Crucible is built on the site of which public house?	
10	What German city is twinned with Sheffield?	
11	Who invented Old Sheffield Plate?	
12	John George Graves opened what in Sheffield in 1934?	
13	Sheffield Wednesdays first match was against who?	
14	Bassett's is famous for making what type of "Allsort"?	
15	In which year did Sheffield become a city?	
16	Sheffield Wednesday first paid their footballers how much for home games in April 1887?	
17	Whose club motto is "by Wisdom and Courage"?	
18	St Paul's Gardens was renamed in 1985 to what?	
19	Was Sheffield Parkway opened in 1964 or 1974?	
20	What king is named on the statue in Fitzalan Square?	

Tiebreaker: The Goodwin fountain has how many jets?

Factoid: Sheffield's first station was the Wicker station. It was opened on the 31st of October 1838.

Answer Page

Big Sheffield Quiz

1) The Blades
2) Hadfield's weir
3) Graves Park
4) Crucible Theatre
5) Larch
6) Ice Hockey
7) Rare Breeds
8) 1997
9) River Porter
10) Town Hall Extension
11) The Owls
12) Fish - Salmon
13) Concord Park
14) 1968
15) Brightside Weir
16) Painted Fabrics
17) The Chartist Group
18) Darnall
19) 12th and 15th Dec.
20) Queen Victoria
21) Hallam FM
22) 1908
23) Victoria Quays
24) 02-05-2003
25) The Full Monty
26) Michael Palin
27) Parson Cross
28) Woodhouse
29) 1864
30) 1982
31) Joe Cocker
32) Cobweb bridge
33) A57
34) Prince Naseem
35) John Wesley
36) Killamarsh
37) Bus, Train, Tram
38) H. Henderson
39) Two road tiers
40) The Sharks
41) Human League
42) 1999
43) Elm Tree

Big Sheffield Quiz

44) Vulcan
45) 1832
46) A Fountain
47) Crystal Peaks
48) Ringinglow
49) Robert Marnock
50) The Lions
51) 1937
52) Crown of Thorns
53) 1624
54) Children's Shelter
55) In front of the Winter garden
56) Mayoress
57) Endcliffe Park
58) Goodwin Fountain
59) 2001
60) 1857
61) Mary queen of Scots
62) Low Edges
63) Fitzalan Square
64) The Blunt Family
65) Thomas de Furnival
66) 30 Acres
67) 1904
68) Human League
69) Parliamentary Forces
70) One stack
71) Eight
72) Blue
73) St. Peter & St. Paul
74) Fish Tank
75) 1893
76) Dixon Lane
77) A large model cow
78) Botanical gardens
79) Bears
80) Queen Victoria

The Car Quest

1) 444
2) Eight
3) Eggbert - Dragon
4) A white toll-gate
5) J.Thomson – A folded guide to amphibians
6) 22-6-1911
7) Godfrey Sykes in 1824 in Malton
8) 1873
9) 8814
10) Radio Sheffield
11) 50th Anniversary
12) Lion
13) 1887
14) 1797
15) 1897
16) Six stacks
17) Totem Pole
18) 13th Duke of Norfolk
19) 1848

Pub Style Quiz 1

1) Meersbrook park
2) Sculpture
3) 22-5-2003
4) Ice Hockey
5) 1932
6) 1982
7) B.B.Taylor
8) Graves Park
9) Birley
10) Stagecoach
11) 1940
12) Cutlery
13) The Full Monty
14) H.Henderson
15) The Crucible
16) May 1943
17) The "Egg Box"
18) 1905
19) Sheffield Flood
20) Def Leopard

Tie Breaker – 39,814

Who, What, Where & When

1) Tilt-Hammer
2) 11-01-04
3) The Lyceum
4) Endcliffe Park
5) Upper Chapel
6) Cocker's
7) Tudor Square
8) The weather
9) Victoria Quay's
10) Western Bank
11) Queen Victoria
12) John Wesley
13) A57
14) James mason
15) Old Queens Head

Five Weirs Quest

1) Queen Victoria
2) Walk Mill Weir
3) 1999
4) Orange tip
5) Cobweb Bridge
6) Four
7) Thomas W.Ward
8) 1856
9) Salmon – Fish
10) 1908
11) 98
12) Walter Spencer
13) 1/3 of a mile
14) Gudgeon, Chubb
15) George Talbot
16) Sir R.Hadfield
17) Pill Box or Guardhouse
18) Abysinnia Br.
19) Heron
20) Brightside Weir
21) Newton Chambers & Co
22) 10
23) Bus,train, S.tram
24) 2
25) 2

46

Sheffield Drinkers Dialect: - "Gerrusanuther"
translates to-   **"Please get me another one"**